When Desire

Meets Freedom

#WontHeDoIt

Samone Allen

Samone Allen

PUBLISHING

Samone Allen

In Loving Memory Of
Mrs. Earline "Big Ma" Harris
April 30, 1916 - September 18, 2006

In Loving Memory Of
Annette "Blood Pressure" Harris
August 18, 1961 - November 1, 1987

Samone Allen

Acknowledgments

I just want to take the time to thank each and every person who has been a part of my life through every heartbreak and every celebration. My life hasn't been a crystal stair, but I definitely give all thanks to the man above for allowing me to see another day. I will not begin naming names because so many people have blessed me along the way and are responsible for getting me to the place where I am in now. I just pray and hope all that read this book will be inspired to keep going even in the midst of any problems you may face. Life does get hard and sometimes even hard to understand but there is no reason to give up on life because God is not going to allow you to fight any battle alone. I want to encourage you to continue to hold to God's unchanging hand and find the desires of your heart.

Samone Allen

Dedication

To My Beautiful Children

You guys are one of the reasons I don't wanna ever give up. You guys push me in different ways you do not even understand. To my first born, Tyler, I am so grateful to raise a son as strong, smart and humble as you. You make me proud every day. To know that your proudest moment was finally seeing me happy just melted my heart. You have been with me for the majority of my life when things were so unclear, and I was just trying my hardest to stay strong and become a great mom. Continue to be who you are and never let anyone steal your joy. To my daughter Londyn, I am just glad God gave me a child with a sense of humor and as nurturing as you. I often look at you and see myself all over again. Continue to put smiles on people's faces because it truly brightens their day. To my four new bonus children, God knew exactly what brings joy to my heart. The personalities and characters of all of you brings tears to my eyes because I am beyond overjoyed to call you my children as well. I pray all my children will read this book and learn not only how to make the right choices but allow God to lead and guide you throughout life. I love you forever.

Samone Allen

To My Sisters, Mona-Lisa "Tutu" and Samantha

We are truly the "Charlie Angels" of our family. We all have and are still going through different challenges but neither one of us lost sight of the faith in which Big Ma has taught us. I love all the times we get together and reminisce on all the memories that we went through living with Big Ma. Our moments are not only great for laughter together but bring healing to the pain we have so deep within. To my big little sis, Tu-Tu, continue to soar forward with your sense of humor and brighten up people's lives; continue to give them strength even when they are ready to give up. Thank you for your service during your time in the military. Continue to be who you are and keep God first in your life. To my twin, my backbone, my alter-ego, my only one call away, Samantha I just want you to continue being you. You are so strong and brave, always going the extra mile. You spoil your nieces and nephews and it's just a delight to have a sister that has my back whenever I need and regardless of whatever I am going through. I love you both forever!

To My Husband, Nick

If God would have shown me my future at 10 years old, I still don't think I would have believed that you would be my soul mate. You complete me and really add the spice to my life that compliments my personality. Thank you for seeing my vision, being my support and just for being a listener. You always give me great words of wisdom. You always allow God to lead you and you constantly remind me how to reach back and find God for answers. I pray that God continues to manifest in our life. I know that this life with you is just the beginning of our testimony as one and our ministry to others. Continue to be who you are because you are a great friend, brother, father, colleague, and humble person; but most of all you are a wonderful *husband* and I am forever grateful. **Love you until death do us apart!**

Samone Allen

When Desire Meets Freedom

This book is an inspirational for young girls as well as adult women that go through different phases of life. As a young girl we are immature to what lies ahead in our future. We are even naive at times because although we see bad things happen, we tend to think – *"It's not going to happen to me."* At a young age, we think that we are smart and making the right choices. However, this book identifies a young woman who was lost at birth and felt like she was in a maze that kept leading to a wall. It was the prayers and God-fearing strength of her grandmother and the introduction of Christ through choir that allowed her to find the desires to her freedom. So many different challenges happened along the way, but she never lost sight of God and remained full of prayer and strength even when she thought that she was weak. It was at the moment of meeting her husband, God sent a message through him to give her the peace and freedom within her heart she needed to heal those wounds. #WONTHEDOIT

Samone Allen

Contents

Samone Allen

Chapter One

"SEEK HIM!"

As a child you are brought into this world, with no worries. You come into this world with no knowledge of who's good or bad. You are just born, fully innocent with pure hope. I felt a little lucky because I came into this world with someone. So I felt a lot of times that I wasn't as alone as most are. I had someone right beside me doing the exact same thing. It wasn't until I was, maybe, 1st grade when I felt that something was missing. I felt like I had missed something. I felt like I did not have the full story of my life. I began to think that the world that I had come to know really was not reality for me. I wondered, *"Am I supposed to be here? Why is everyone's mother so much younger than my Big Ma. Where did all this family come from?"* So many questions going on, day after day. It was pure innocence of wondering how I was created. No one had really given me all the story or even seemed to know all of the facts of my existence. There I was, young, and crying more than I can even remember smiling. I was always crying because I missed something. I was crying for the unknown, so I thought. It was the creation of me in which I felt was gone. There was no memory, only a picture. A picture of a memory that I felt like I needed help to understand. I constantly found myself looking at this picture. I felt like I once knew the person in the picture. It was a picture I still now feel is only a memory; one that so many other people once knew also. That picture, that one picture, allowed me to envision who the person was. When I finally found out that the person in the picture was the woman who created me, I felt lost all over again. I didn't know how to accept it. I was too young, so I thought. The reality left me distraught. It did not seem right for anyone to leave this world before raising their own creations. This world should not work like this. I needed more answers to understand. Most children have a way of acting out when something is wrong. It's common because many times you don't understand your own emotions, better yet know how to react to them. In my case, I "acted out" by crying; I just cried and cried. Someone would only fuss at me and I would be an emotional wreck. I was still searching for answers to make my life make sense. I felt like it was just so unfair.

I didn't get answers, instead I found myself in the care of a lady named "Big Ma." I feel this woman was the strongest woman to ever live on this earth. She was my grandmother, but I had to learn that she wasn't just a woman raising me, she was a God-fearing strong woman. She made the decision to not only raise my two sisters and I, but she decided this at 70 years of age after she had already raised *twenty-two* of her own kids. She sacrificed so much for us. I don't even think many people in today's world would make the sacrifices that she made. She was a woman that knew that our world would not be as easy as we thought. She saw that we would be used by Satan even before we knew who Satan was. She saw that we would be very vulnerable, so she was extremely strict and hard on us. If I knew what she was doing before now, I don't think I would have been as slick at the mouth nor felt like she was just plain ole' strict.

Let's rewind for a minute because as a child I was the quietest of all the three of us. Having a twin, I've always felt like she is my alter-ego. She is the one that is small but acts as if she is as big as a giant. She is the type that if five people wanted to fight her, she would go for it. She is also very sneaky as well. My grandmother always used to fuss at her because she knew when she was up to something. If we went into a store my grandmother always kept her closer to her because she knew she would wonder. Lord forbid if it's some other kids our age there, she is making a friend for sure. There are so many stories about my twin that I laugh about now, but at the time being raised by Big Ma, I cried through. My grandmother didn't just whoop one person for what they did, she whooped all. We were twins, so I guess she thought we were supposed to do everything together and whoopings were part of it. Then I had my older sister as well; she was probably the most outspoken out of us, as we were younger. It may be a tie between my twin and her because both of them are something else. I can remember my oldest sister got a whooping every day after school. My twin and I would just look at each other like, *"What in the world did she do at school?"* She made us think going to "big kids'" school would have you getting whoopings in the evenings because that was routine for my grandmother and her. We were in Head Start at the time, so we were trying to stay in Head Start as long as we could. If I can remember, I think I cried so hard at my Head Start graduation because I was not ready for my oldest sister's life. Now, I was not the perfect child because my grandmother would fuss a lot at me however, she could be very personal and say hurtful things in regard to the lady in the picture. When she made statements like that, it was the only time I would speak out because as I stated earlier, I did not know the one in the picture she spoke about. I was sensitive to the whole ordeal of my life. However the things she said I would always stand up telling her I would not be like the person in the picture. I wanted her to know I was going to be a smart girl. I was going to do the right thing. I never liked for my grandmother to say any words that would degrade who I was or would be. So yes, I used to go back and forth with my grandmother. Now let me tell you - do not for once think talking back to any adult, especially the one raising you, is a great idea to do. I knew the consequences would not be great, but I was hurt and tired of crying. Here I was in this world where I was still trying to understand what I was living in. It was just too much for an emotional person like me to take.

We all took our situation differently and no matter how old we got, we all handled it much different. See, I know you are probably wondering what happened, who really was the person in the picture. The lady in the picture was our mother. She was beautiful and very athletic, from what I was told. She was red headed, with a nice gap in her teeth and legs perfect and muscular for any runner. She was the youngest girl of my grandmother's children. To many she was a friend, a sister, a teammate, a classmate and a relative. For my sisters and I she was just a memory. I can maybe say for my twin sister and I that she was just a picture.

We never got the chance to even know how she looked because she was killed when we were only a year old. Our older sister was 4 years old at the time and was able to spend just a little more time on earth with her, but of course a lot of her memory faded because she was so young. The story was told that someone came to the apartment where my mother and her roommate lived in Gary, Indiana. She opened the door and a gunshot to her head killed her on the spot. Her roommate jumped out the window and even this day, is still blind from that jump. It was said that my sisters and I were in the next room asleep during the time this happened. See, my mother was living what they call the *"fast life."* She did drugs and she drank alcohol; she was just what we call today "living." To this day we don't even know who our dad(s) is/are because she was really *"living the life."* There were times when we were left alone and without food. I was told I was the baby who just cried and cried, and the lady across the hall would come get us. My grandmother had made many trips up to Gary and tried her hardest to get our mother on the narrow path. However, as a mother, she only could do what she knew how and that was to pray over her child. After my mother died, my grandmother took guardianship over us. However, prior to that, we had been to different foster homes and children shelters even before we got to our grandmother. Soon, after a few months we moved to Mississippi. This was nothing but God's doing to even give my grandmother the strength to be able to take us all in. So, see, my grandmother was more than just a grandmother, she was "My Mother".

The scripture says "People are born for trouble as readily as sparks fly up from a fire. If I were you, I would go to God and present my case to him. He does great things too marvelous to understand." (Job 5:7-9)

These versus shows me the direction I should be going. I was seeking answers from people on this Earth that did not have the answers.

See, all this time I was looking for answers about the woman in the picture when all my answers were right in front of me. God already knew the plan even before I was born. He knew my concerns and He knew my pain. All I had to do was trust God and seek Him. Everything else would just unfold. As I stated earlier, I was lost - but my grandmother already knew this. I look back now and see how she made sure that we were involved in different mentorship programs, for example - one in particular called, *"Our House, Inc."* It was filled with other children just like my sisters and I, or similar. They too had lost their loved ones due to different situations. However, that program had mentors and spiritual leaders to give us all the hope we needed to move forward and create goals. My grandmother knew she needed other outlets to help us learn how to cope with tragedy and traumatic situations. She knew she had to be strong and a faithful servant of God and do His will raising us. She knew her purpose and the reason she was still on this earth. **"Train up a child in the way he should go: and when he is old, he will not depart from it." (Proverbs 22:6)**

She would pray over us at night and anoint us with oil throughout the night. She instilled in us how to seek answers from God with just a prayer and to call on His name. I will not say being young is an excuse to not seek God because all you have to do is call His name. He will hear your cry. As I grew older and started seeking God, I and everyone else could see how my life started brightening up. I had no choice but to *smile*! God had delivered me long before I knew; and as I said, He continued to give strength to my grandmother to raise my sisters and I. He wanted to give us a life that we would gain lessons from and receive His teachings through. He wanted us to know Him, and I am forever grateful.

Samone Allen

Chapter Two

"I'm On Another Day's Journey"

It's like heaven to my ears when I hear the sweet sounds of music. It's not just hearing music, it's the percussions, the cymbals, the tambourine, the piano, the clapping, the feet stomp, the altos, the tenors and the sopranos that you have no choice but to stand and give God praise to the music that comes together as one ministry. My grandmother took us to church at least 6 days out of the 7-day week. You would think that this is a lot for me. I must be honest – of course, being so young going to church just about *every single da*y, yes - I thought she was over doing it. I really thought it was punishment because I was like, *"Do we really need this much church?"* I am sure that sounded naive and that's just what it was. I was so immature to what God was setting me up for that I felt like church was boring and not for me. As I got a little older, I eventually started understanding.

I was about 5 or 6 years old and my grandmother pretty much wanted to turn my sisters and I into a gospel singing group. There was a that lady she knew around the corner that taught music and trained our voice. My grandmother would send us around to her house once or twice a week for practice. Now, the only thing I was not fond of going to this house was that she had a dog. My sisters and I were too scared of dogs even though we had hunting dogs of our own. It was times we would tell a fib to our grandmother saying we had already gone to the lady's house when we really didn't, only because we were not trying to play bite-catch with the dog. I am here to tell you that telling my grandmother fibs was not the best course of action. When she found out that we were not telling the truth, we would look at each other with tears and we already knew, as one famous comedian would say, *"IT'S ABOUT TO GO DOWN!"*

After it all went down, we finally got focused and started singing. We went from singing at one church to singing at 3-5 churches. We were singing our most favorite song called *"On Another Day's Journey"*. That was one of our most popular songs that we sung, and we would have the whole church up on their feet and the mother board shouting! Singing the song *"On Another Days Journey"* was deeper than the words that were sung. Every day we are blessed to wake up and we are on a journey. Some people make it through the whole day of the journey, and some do not. Every day that I am able to start fresh, I cannot do anything else but give God the glory. I am glad we chose that song as one of our most famous songs to sing together as sisters. I feel as though this song is what led us to the journey of singing for God. We even had a pianist whom we called our godbrother. He was a very well-rounded and known pianist, so we pretty much went where he went. We sang as sisters until we were about 9 or 10 years old and then we ran into this youth choir that we were eager to join because of how good they sounded. My grandmother was overjoyed that we wanted to join the choir. She wanted us to be part of a positive influence which included singing for God. When we joined that choir, I felt that's when the life of singing for God really hit me. The ministry of singing for God was not in error that my grandmother saw for us. It was just the beginning of how God was going to minister to me.

When you get in choirs so young, you kind of see it as just an every Sunday thing that you do, possibly that your parents/guardian made you do in the church. However, this was a different type of choir because it represented a community. It was a small community, with loud voices. This showed me it did not matter how old or young you were, you could bring someone closer to God through song. From the moment I heard this choir, that is definitely what that it did. Singing in that choir you would laugh, you would cry, you would travel, you created relationships and most importantly - the Holy Spirit would take over. I really enjoyed the experience at such a young age because even when I would go through difficult things in life such as school, I could reconnect with this choir when we went to rehearsal or choir performances and something would move on the inside me that would bring me to tears. I must say I cried quite a bit because I was filled with so many emotions and personal things that even going to God seemed like so much to bear.

"Make a joyful noise unto the Lord, all ye lands. Serve the Lord with gladness: come before his presence with singing. Know Ye that the Lord he is God. It is he that hath made us, and not we ourselves; we are his people and the sheep of his pasture. Enter into his gates with thanksgiving and into his courts with praise: be thankful unto him, and bless his name. For the Lord is good; His mercy is everlasting and his truth endureth to all generations." (Psalms 100:1-5)

I remember times when my grandmother would sit on the front row at every church and she would shout and give a testimony that always touched me. I always cried because she was doing her best at raising us and there were things that I still didn't understand that she would testify about. I mean, if you lost your child and had to raise your grandchildren that's a big responsibility. The very thought of carrying the weight of healing from your 22- year old daughter being killed and no longer on this earth is burden enough. I have trouble dealing with death, whether I knew you or not. It's just hard to process especially when it's someone so close and you tried your best to help and pray things would get better, so I can only imagine how Big Ma felt.

The greatest thing about gospel songs is they have many spiritual meanings and powerful words creating spiritual guidance and testimony. I am sure the Holy Spirit moved through my grandmother through so many songs.

My sisters and I continued singing with another community choir that my godbrother soon started years later. Currently my oldest sister still sings with his choir to this day. I am forever grateful for these community choirs that I sang with my entire youth and adult years because it really helped me cope with things when I didn't know where to turn. Singing in a choir isn't just plain singing, it's a ministry. You never know whose life is changing through the songs. The hardest thing that I am sure many gospel singers fight with is how to sing when you are going through. See the thing about singing for God is that you are not perfect but even in your imperfections, because you are yielding yourself as a tool to God - the enemy will acknowledge that before acknowledging you singing for God. I know this because the enemy was always around, even when I didn't even know. However, my hope still in singing was that God would use me to turn any person's life around, as I worked on myself.

Before I go any further, I do not want you to think that singing in the choir is the only way to be blessed or even live for God. Music in general is just a great gift where you have a platform to create positivity to help the next person get through another day. There are so many opportunities to become the person God has ordained you to be. This is when you find your purpose in life. Every person has a gift and some gifts become your career, your hobby, or simply a gift used when needed. The only thing about gifts from God, you never want to waste a gift. Also, you are never too old to find your purpose and use your gift. There is no age stamped on things God has planned for you. I had to learn that over the years. True enough my grandmother started me singing but there was a bigger picture going on that God wanted my sisters and I to experience. I am still working on my purpose and gift from God.

So, do I wish my grandmother would have allowed us to do what we wanted as kids other than sing in choirs? Not at all do I wish that. For the most part, I really enjoyed being involved in the community through these choirs. Every day was a journey for me in my eyes. As a kid, I was always wondering, *"What's going to happen next."*

More than anything, I'm grateful because the seeds planted during these years literally became the pinnacle of strength for me. These seeds would be responsible for saving my life when I was face to face with hurt, pain, and murder.

Samone Allen

Chapter 3

"Never Would Have Made It"

The time had finally come after all the choir practices, school projects, Easter dresses, proms, early Saturday morning pressing comb days, and disciplining punishments; it was now time for high school graduation. My grandmother used to always tell us she prayed the prayer for God to let her live until all three of us graduated. Well she made it and we graduated. I graduated at the top 20 of my high school class of over 500 students. It was one of the happiest days of my life; I was accomplishing something that I looked forward to since elementary. Of course, by this time I thought I was ready for the world or to "be grown," as they say. I had been accepted into an HBCU (Historical Black College & Universities) college and had a job. I was on my way to success to obtain a career.

My first year of college went well. It was full of fun and I met a lot of different people; I was enjoying life as a college student. I had so many friends attending college with me and I felt really blessed because if they had anything, I had it as well. It was going really great until my second semester of college. My grandmother started getting really sick. She was diagnosed with cancer. I withdrew from school and went back home. I wanted to help her around the house and help her to get around where she needed to go such as doctor appointments and grocery store runs. I ended up going to a college near our hometown and worked as much as I could.

Luckily, I had an aunt that worked in the health field. She would come every day after work and help take care of my grandmother and show us how to make her comfortable. We were young, so my family wanted us to ensure we continued to live our lives and finish school. I decided that next fall that I would enroll back into the HBCU college I started at.

I went back to college that following fall semester and she died a month later in September. I truly was lost for words and a part of my heart died as well. I cried all night and day after I received the news. All I could wonder was, "What do I do now? Where will I go when it's time to go where I called home?" It was just so many things I had on my mind, I felt I had lost everything before my eyes. I must say I would beat myself up because I felt like I should have been there when she took her last breath. God knew best because after it was all said and done, she made it pass what she asked God.

I continued college after my grandmother's passing and tried to get back focused on what I needed to do to graduate. Well, let's just say that was the plan - but things started falling apart before my eyes. When I thought I was taking two steps forward, it was like I was moving three steps back. I started working three jobs along with being in school full-time. I had a car note and cell phone, so I felt I needed the jobs to ensure I was able to manage since I really didn't have anyone to financially assist me. Everything was going well but like majority of focused girls, we have the heart of gold. We fill empty spaces with maybe what we think is love and finding out too late it's only lust. I had been dating this guy since senior year of high school. This was the first guy my grandmother even allowed to go pass the screen door. He was the one that could call the phone in his regular voice without having to call a friend on three-way to ask for me. With that being said, I felt with my grandmother's approval, I was on the right track. Life just seemed like things were going in the right direction. I was working, going to school, and thought I had found love. It wasn't long before I was wondering if love came with hurt and bruises. I wondered, "Is this what I'm supposed to tell my future kids? Am I supposed to care that he lies and cheats?"

So many questions were going on in my mind, on top of facing other personal things in my life. I just became numb and naive to everything. I was like I was a zombie, going to work and going to school. Months passed and soon had a full-time job, I was still a full-time student, I had an apartment, a car note, and bills. The grown person that I was trying to become came quicker than I had planned. It wasn't months later after that when I then became pregnant too. *"Lord, if you can hear my cry please*

Lord come and deliver me." This was my cry out in all my prayers during this time because I didn't know what to do. I was simply existing - until my first wakeup call came. I got off work one day and it was raining extremely hard. I was very tired and ready to get home. My apartment wasn't too far from my job so I took the interstate so that I could get there quicker. Within seconds I went through this large puddle of water on the interstate and hydroplaned across three lanes and stopped by the median. I stopped within a tenth of a second of an 18-wheeler passing by. I started crying immediately and two ladies stopped to help; they were looking shocked but made sure I was okay. They said *"Wow, you were this close to that truck!"* I looked, trying to see if I had hit anyone else. I hadn't hit anybody, and nobody had hit me. This interstate is usually very busy - all the time, so to know I basically walked out of this accident with just soreness was breathtaking. Well just know I had a short time to take that breath before I was faced with another battle. The words of *"If it's not one thing, it's another."* came within a blink of an eye.

I never would've imagined one day getting off work, going to school, eating out and then going back home would be more than a memory. It was a memory that I had to recall instantly from every breath I took, every step I took, and every word I said. It was like being in a nightmare and no matter how much water I put on my face - I couldn't wake up. This story was like something you read about or just hear about, not something you really have to live through, much less plead your innocence through.

I should've known something was wrong when I got a call that morning from my boyfriend's ex-girlfriend's roommate asking where I was. It was a completely different type of call. Later that day I was at work and it showed up on television that his ex-girlfriend was missing. My heart felt like it just broke into millions of pieces. I went to the breakroom crying and could barely get words out trying to understand, as my co-worker braced me with hugs and tears. Anyone who had a heart couldn't help but hurt because, like I said, no one expects something like this to happen so close to home. Days and weeks were going by and still nothing, and no sign of this ex-girlfriend. I was trying my best to pull myself together, going to work and trying to go to school - trying to continue my day-to-day. Giving encouraging words and trying to be strong for my boyfriend because I was knowing that he still cared about her; there is no way I would think he didn't care. I also was pregnant as well, so I had to continue to be strong for myself as well. Of course the police were constantly questioning me during this time and while I was overwhelmed, I had opened doors because I had nothing to hide.

When Desire Meets Freedom: #WontHeDoIt

I am a very honest person, my friends and family will all tell you to never tell me secrets because I simply can't "hold water," as the old folks say. Not only that, I wanted her to be found. I wanted it to be one of those moments for her where may you just needed some alone time. In my heart, I just needed her to be okay. I went home for a few days because I needed to be around my family. I resigned from my job and stopped going to school. I needed some peace of mind for myself. More than anything, I needed a sign from God.

The daily prayers I was doing, I just didn't feel like I was saying the right prayer. Had I gotten so far from God where I couldn't hear? I finally asked my aunt to set up a private prayer session for myself and my boyfriend. We went the following day and my aunt's pastor and wife, whom I had known since I was able to walk in the church, prayed over us. We sat on our knees at the altar as they prayed, and tears just rolled down my eyes. As I looked over to my boyfriend, he was in deep cries almost louder than the pastor. At that moment, I was in complete shock and looked with wondering eyes and just said, *"Lord help him."* I had never seen him like that. The pastor then read a scripture:

"If you declare with your mouth, "Jesus is Lord," and believe in your heart that God raised him from the dead, you will be saved. For it is with

your heart that you believe and are justified, and it is with your mouth

that you profess your faith and are saved." (Romans 10:9-10)

One of the few things the pastor's wife stated before we left was, *"In three days, everything will come to the light."* The next day he confessed to the murder of his ex-girlfriend when he went to a court hearing. I couldn't believe it. I was like, "I gotta watch the news first," because when people began calling me, I was just in zombie mode again. I finally saw the news and just couldn't believe what I was seeing nor what I was hearing. One of my aunts and uncles came over to my aunt's house to talk to me and I told them everything through tears. I was just so naive and dumb because I had no idea; I was simply blinded. If it was a snake it would have bit me. My uncle in tears, Lord rest his soul, said to me *"Girl, it could've been you too.".* They hugged me and embraced me, and we all were in tears. A mirror coincidence that is even more eerie - the same day that my mom was killed was also the same day this young lady, my boyfriend's ex-girlfriend, went missing. To bring even more chills to my soul - my mom's murderer was identified the same day that hers was. Pain just stabbed my heart over and over as I tried to find comfort. My heart was filled with so much trauma.

After a few weeks, my twin sister came, got me, and took me with her to Atlanta. As we drove, a song came on and just put me in a different set of tears. The song said, *"I never would've made it!"* I felt my strength shifting and my heart renewing to a different mindset to think and even live. I knew that life wasn't definitely going to be easy after the last few weeks I had lived through. Back to back, year after year almost within the same timeframe, souls left this cruel world and here I was once again lost trying to find my purpose. Why was *my life* filled with so many trials and tribulations? As I looked at myself in the mirror, I felt weak, even when I thought I was being strong.

As I looked in the mirror and looked down below my chest, all I knew was that God had a gift in store for me. I knew I had to provide for my child and become stronger, even when I felt the weakest. From then on, I looked at things as only a test of my faith; all I had to do is keep the faith.

Samone Allen

Chapter 4

"Lord Make Me Over"

One of my favorite ways to cook is to cook from scratch. It simply tastes better to me and makes me feel like I am cooking with my grandma. Well that's how I felt my life was going as well. I had to start from scratch again. I felt I needed to stop allowing the world to direct me to where I need to go and stop depending on people. It was much easier said than done, I might add. No matter how much God was on my side, Satan was not giving up either. He wanted to see if I learned my lessons or if I even care about myself. I was 3-6 months pregnant looking for a job and just trying to figure out what was next for us. My twin sister was right at my hip, not letting me give up on myself. My oldest sister was in Iraq during this time and my twin sister was really the only person helping as much as she could. I finally got a job and was able to get Georgia Medicaid to begin seeing a doctor. I was truly blessed because my pregnancy was very smooth throughout all the trauma and depression I was going through. I eventually moved back home once again, because I knew nothing about raising a child or what to do and my twin sister worked a lot, so I needed some support.

I moved back and stayed with my aunt that was in the health field once again. She is God sent, I promise, because she was just like the mother you would need when your child is pregnant. She wanted me to be strong, eat daily and keep her informed of all my changes. It was my first child and therefore I was having all types of emotions going on, not to mention only a box of pampers. My aunt was doing what she could, and I didn't have a job – so I had no finances to buy anything. My sister finally came back from Iraq and took me on a baby shopping spree. I put everything in the basket that I thought I needed! There were other family and friends who helped as well. As the song says, "*He is on time God*!" and that's just what I thought to myself. I finally had my son a week later after my due date and delivered a 9lbs 4oz baby boy. I thought to myself, "*Like wow, he is perfect.*" My aunt and my son's grandmother were my support system for the first few months after delivering my son. I started back going to my old church, had a job and was singing with the community choir again. Everything was slowly getting back to where I felt I knew who I was again. I then moved back to Atlanta with my twin sister. My hours had dropped to PRN at my job at the time, so I wanted to go in a different direction and try to find my purpose.

What I thought would have changed my life for the better of moving back to Atlanta turned out to be one of my most struggling times. My sister was in between jobs and I couldn't get a job. We only had one car that my oldest sister gave us, so I let my twin use the car because I wasn't working. Trying to get government assistance in Georgia was one of the hardest times of my life because if you weren't there before the birds started chirping then you were out of luck. If you didn't have all the paperwork you needed at your visit, you still were out of luck. I then began job searching. I had no babysitter, so my son was right there at every application filling. Every day I would grab my son's diaper bag and fill it up with pampers and food. I would walk like eight miles to the nearest library with my son in his stroller. My son had a tan, but he was still smiling like nothing even mattered. My sister and I then began working at a club trying to make ends meet. My god-cousin babysit for me, thankfully, while I worked. After a few months of the job not paying well, bills began to pile up and we soon got evicted.

My twin sister went to stay with a friend, and I stayed at one of my mother's neighborhood friend's vacant rental houses. I stayed there for about two weeks - then moved out and went to some of my god-aunt houses near Columbus, GA. I must say I was on the move trying to find myself. Going from house to house and city to city trying to get myself back on track and self-sufficient to take care of my child. I was at church one Sunday in Columbus and it all came to me. The church was having some type of scholarship fundraising program and the message made me feel like they were talking directly to me. I went home and immediately looked up information to get back in school. I called my oldest sister and asked her to send me some gas money to get back to Atlanta because one of my cousins had a check for me that came to her mom's house. The check was just enough to get me back to Mississippi and pay my deposit to get into the school's apartments.

I moved back and I was able to return to school, work, and find daycare services for my son. Everything just worked itself out. I soon started to date again once things began to look clearer. The new "Trey Songz" album had come out and I was "*Ready*", lol. I was ready to fall in love and just finish my "*happily ever after.*" That is when I connected with my daughter's father. I knew him from my hometown, and we used to hang out a little before my grandmother passed. We experienced the "honeymoon stage" for about a year. We got an apartment together with one of my closest friends whom I called "*little big brother*" and soon, I became pregnant with my daughter. Unfortunately, this pregnancy put me out of work. I had to be out on leave a whole six months for a "placenta previa." I was not happy because that was my last semester before graduation, and I was determined to finish. Thankfully, my teachers really worked with me and I am forever grateful because that could've put me back a semester. Being out of work with kids to support was very hard. I thank God that my daughter's father was blessed with a decent career and that we received so much support from close friends and family.

On April 28, 2012, I completed a milestone and a dream. I received my bachelor's degree. It was one of those life changing events that gives you more than strength. It was that *"never would have made it"* type of accomplishment. Some things get accomplished in life and some just don't for whatever reason, but there is a scripture that allows things to supersede all hopes and dreams. The scriptures say,

"But I rejoiced in the Lord greatly that now at last your care for me has flourished again; though you surely did care, but you lacked opportunity. Not that I speak in regard to need, for I have learned in whatever state I am, to be content: I know how to be abased, and I know how to abound. Everywhere and in all things I have learned both to be full and to be hungry, both to abound and to suffer need. I can do all things through Christ who strengthens me."

(Philippians 4:10-13 NKJV)

From deep depression, to losing focus of who and what was important in this life, I was sure that it wasn't the end of my going through things but accomplishing goals even when the enemy had planned other alternate routes was major for me. I am glad that I always remembered who will always put me on top. I had graduated, had two kids and overcome many trials. I felt like it was time to focus on me. I believed it was time to start my career. I also thought that family and marriage would be another good idea. Well, of course none of that happened the way I wanted. I got all big headed before I knew it, thinking I was supposed to have something before consulting God. My expectations were far past what He had in store.

On the bright side, I graduated looking for a job and found a job within minor of Industrial Technology. I was grateful still, even though the job wasn't in my major. I became a Quality Supervisor for about 4 years at a car manufacturer. I was beyond blessed because the field I wanted to work in before I dropped out of college was the career that I still ended up in. This chapter in my life really turned out better than I expected. God didn't give up on me and He never left my side. I always ended back on top where I left off before the struggle.

Samone Allen

Chapter 5

"Won't He Do It"

There are many times where we are simply overloaded with stress, thoughts, pain, and sadness that we simply need to get some fresh air. In November 2016, I realized I needed some fresh air. I needed to be rejuvenated and just filled with the selfishness of loving *myself* for a change. I had moved back to Atlanta once again, following my fiancé' (at the time) and still was not happy with myself. Things were not as smooth as they once were with him and I realize that it was time to just cut ties. I needed to be rejuvenated and filled with the selfishness of loving myself. I decided that at the top of the year 2017 I was moving to Florida. Why Florida? I always felt like Florida was the vacation place – the place to relax; so I moved to there. I received my tax return at the end of February and March 1st, it was, "*Jacksonville here I come!*" The kids were still in school and I didn't want them to leave school towards the end of the year so they stayed with my daughter's father until the end of the school year. This was a critical moment in my life and one that many women don't get to experience.

I made it to Florida, and I could just smell the waves from the beach. I would go to the beach daily and walk the brim of the ocean for 7 to 8 miles while listening to music. Then sometimes I would walk, talk to God, and just look at all the things I'd been through. While sometimes it made me cry, I felt the majority of the time I began smiling just as much. I felt deep down

I was becoming my smile. As a mother, my children not only needed to see me smile, they needed to feel it as well. See, what I needed to learn is to not be content with life. I needed to understand what God had done for me was not done for me to just settle for contentment. All the crying I was doing was not normal for someone that was blessed. I was often reminded by my best friend how important it was for me to smile. She always communicated with me how to create a balance to make myself happy. She was a friend that really gave it to me straight and I feel like she had a ministry of her own that really inspired me to continue and face things that I sometimes dodged on purpose.

It only took looking in the mirror and trying to see who I really was that changed everything. I began working out, treating myself and just having fun. Now it was not as perfect as it sounded, nor easy. However, just know that everything began coming to slowly but surely. Music being a huge component of my core, I soon found another song that reminded me that everything that the enemy planned for my downfall would produce my greatest victories. It also reminded me that God was the only one that would make things right, and that He would *always* show up.

It wasn't long before the words of "*Won't He Do It*" became part of my everyday language. I became high for what the Lord had planned for me. My smile was like a flower, it was blossoming every time you saw me. There was nothing fake about my smile because I knew what I had been through and I had nothing left *except* my smiles. I started smiling more because I wanted to rub off some of the love that God had on me to someone else who also may have needed a smile. It wasn't much longer, a man came to me and told me to never let anyone become in control of my happiness. I wasn't so sure of what he meant at first because I didn't even really understand what he was saying. Sometimes we don't realize when God speaks but at that moment, I knew that was a message from God. He didn't want me any longer to enjoy temporary happiness. He wanted me to be able to look in the mirror and recognize who I was, and to be happy about it. When I started doing that, oh boy, shower of blessings rained down! I got up one morning while in Florida and talked to my roommate and told her I wanted to move to Texas. I was working at the time as a Social Worker and I didn't know how to leave my job, because I didn't want to leave on a bad note. I also didn't want to leave my clients and I definitely didn't want to leave on such short notice. My roommate looked at me, got out of bed, went to the computer and began writing my notice for me. LOL! She expressed to me what she had seen in me over the last few months of knowing and living with me. She complimented me on being strong, hard-working and a great mother. She then encouraged me to complete my mission. A week later around the top of August 2017, I moved to Texas. I stayed with some of my close friends for about three months. By my second week, I'd landed an average paying job. A month later I received a call for an interview for a job within the trucking industry. I was so excited because things were going smooth. I was praying, reading my Bible, and just staying humble. I got that job!! In November, I got my first apartment on my own, and made more money than I had ever made in my entire 29 years of life. I was able to take care of my kids and See their smiles and souls become joyful.

But wait... let's rewind for a second because the man who gave me those great words of wisdom from God, well he became my husband. I must say, I never would have seen him coming if God had told me Himself that he was about to shift me into such a new direction. I honestly can say we both thought the same. He is no one perfect, but he is definitely perfect for me. From the time I met him until now the blessings haven't stopped. I feel like I am doing something right and I know I am heading into the right direction. I promised God that I wasn't going to be content, nor would I ignore him. I knew that this man was heaven sent.

I once heard the saying that you will meet your soulmate at least one time in your life and you will never know it. That is definitely true because while I was singing in the choir at 10 or 11 years old, he was right across the street playing ball with his friends. It was a small town, but everyone knew everyone. We reunited after almost 20 years and felt like God had us to reunite within the right time frame. I am forever grateful because we are each other's strength. So often in my past life, I always felt weak when I was going through so many situations. I have someone who fears God, prays for me, prays with me, and is humble. A person like this can only keep you sane, even when you start to get lost or want to give up again.

Now, I am a successful Quality Engineer, have gained four more beautiful children, have a wonderful husband and am a happy wife. This life lets me know that everything I went through - I went through for a reason. God will fight those battles so that you can sleep *without* worries and stress. You definitely have to believe and stay steadfast in your faith. You have to learn your lesson and pray. Reading your Bible and just studying His Word can keep you on the stress-free path. Always remember who you are and destined to be. Never let someone be in control of your happiness, regardless who they are. Listen, when God speaks to you, He does so to help you avoid ignorance and being naive. Always seek God in everything you do. Always honor your parent(s)/guardians and take care of them when they are old. As you travel on this journey, know that in all you do, continue to give thanks to the Lord above. Everything that you go through, you never will *make it* through without God. So when it's all said and done, and you find your happiness - just look in the mirror, lift your hands and say, "*WONT HE DO IT*!!"

"Hear, my children, the instruction of a father, And give attention to know understanding; For I give you good doctrine: Do not forsake my law. When I was my father's son, Tender and the only one in the sight of my mother, He also taught me, and said to me: "Let your heart retain my words; Keep my commands, and live. Get wisdom! Get understanding! Do not forget, nor turn away from the words of my mouth. Do not forsake her, and she will preserve you; Love her, and she will keep you. Wisdom is the principal thing; Therefore get wisdom. And in all your getting, get understanding. Exalt her, and she will promote you; She will bring you honor, when you embrace her. She will place on your head an ornament of grace; A crown of glory she will deliver to you." Hear, my son, and receive my sayings, And the years of your life will be many. I have taught you in the way of wisdom; I have led you in the right paths. When you walk, your steps will not be hindered, And when you run, you will not stumble. Take firm hold of instruction, do not let go; Keep her, foe she is your life. Do not enter the path of the wicked, And do not walk in the way of evil. Avoid it, do not travel on it; Turn away from it and pass on.

For they do not sleep unless they have done evil; And their sleep is taken away unless they make someone fall. For they eat the bread of wickedness,

And drink the wine of violence. But the path of the just is like the shining sun, That shines ever brighter unto the perfect day. The way of the wicked is like darkness;

They do not know what makes them stumble. My son, give attention to my words;

Incline your ear to my sayings. Do not let them depart from your eyes;

Keep them in the midst of your heart; For they are life to those who find them,

And health to all their flesh. Keep your heart with all diligence, For out of it spring the issues of life. Put away from you a deceitful mouth, And put perverse lips far from you.

Let your eyes look straight ahead, And your eyelids look right before you.

Ponder the path of your feet, And let all your ways be established. Do not turn to the right or the left; Remove your foot from evil.
(Phillipians 4:1-27)

When Desire Meets Freedom: #WontHeDoIt

Samone Allen

About the Author

Born Samone Harris, she recently married her wonderful husband, and now goes by the name of Mrs. Samone Allen. Mrs. Allen was born in Gary, Indiana and was raised in Greenville, MS. She is the baby twin sister of two older sisters. She is the mother of six children, two biological and four bonus children. Mrs. Allen graduated an honor student from Greenville-Weston High in 2005. She continued her education at Jackson State University in Mississippi, earning her Bachelor of Social Work degree along with a minor in Industrial Technology. Mrs. Allen currently resides in Dallas, TX with her husband and family.